THE BLACKBERRY BLOSSOM FIDDLE BOOK FOR STRING BASS

Arrangements by Myanna Harvey

Exercises by Cassia Harvey

CHP386

©2020 by C. Harvey Publications All Rights Reserved.

www.charveypublications.com - print books
www.learnstrings.com - PDF downloadable books
www.harveystringarrangements.com - chamber music

Table of Contents

How to Use This Book..................................3

1. Harvest Home: First Warm-Up..................4
2. Harvest Home: Second Warm-Up...............5
3. **Harvest Home**..6
4. Blackberry Blossom: First Warm-Up..................8
5. Blackberry Blossom: Second Warm-Up............9
6. **Blackberry Blossom**..................................10
7. The Dashing Sergeant: First Warm-Up..............12
8. The Dashing Sergeant: Second Warm-Up........13
9. **The Dashing Sergeant**..............................14
10. Old Joe Clark: First Warm-Up........................16
11. Old Joe Clark: Second Warm-Up...................17
12. **Old Joe Clark**...18
13. King of the Fairies: First Warm-Up..................20
14. King of the Fairies: Second Warm-Up.............21
15. **King of the Fairies**..................................22
16. The Blarney Pilgrim: First Warm-Up..................24
17. The Blarney Pilgrim: Second Warm-Up..............25
18. **The Blarney Pilgrim**.................................26
19. The Parting Blessing: Warm-Up......................28
20. **The Parting Blessing**...............................29
21. Leather Breeches: First Warm-Up...................30
22. Leather Breeches: Second Warm-Up..............31
23. **Leather Breeches**...................................32
24. The Rakes of Kildare: First Warm-Up...............34
25. The Rakes of Kildare: Second Warm-Up..........35
26. **The Rakes of Kildare**...............................36
27. Big John McNeil: First Warm-Up.....................38
28. Big John McNeil: Second Warm-Up................39
29. **Big John McNeil**......................................40
30. The Red-Haired Boy: First Warm-Up................42
31. The Red-Haired Boy: Second Warm-Up............43
32. **The Red-Haired Boy**................................44

How to Use This Book on Your Own
- Start by playing the Warm-Up Exercises. The "A" parts are more difficult than the "B" parts and will help you work towards the Advanced Melody on the next page.
- Play the Stress-Free Melody. Work on playing in tune and using quick, precise finger and bow changes.
- Play the Advanced Melody. Start with small sections of 2-4 measures and then work to put them together to form the melody.
- Circle any places where you consistently stop and play two notes before and two notes after the stop, 5 times. Start slowly and gradually get faster until you have thoroughly learned the transition.

How to Use This Book in Private Lessons
- Practice the book on your own, using the suggestions listed above.
- Play the Stress-Free Melody and then the Advanced Melody in a duet with your teacher, who can play the Teacher Harmony. For variety, switch parts with your teacher!

How to Use This Book in a Mixed Instrument and/or Mixed-Level String Class
- The Violin, Viola, Cello, and Bass books can be played and learned together.
- Students at a moderately accomplished or more advanced level can play the Regular Exercise. Students at a basic or beginning level can play the Basic Exercise.
- Moderately accomplished students can play the Stress-Free Melody, more advanced students can play the Advanced Melody, and students at a basic or beginning level can play the Basic Harmony. The teacher can play any of the parts with the students, the Teacher Harmony, or the piano accompaniment.
- **The "A" and "B" parts of each exercise are compatible and can be played together.**
- **All melodies and harmonies for each fiddle tune are compatible and can be played together.**

How to Use This Book in a Small Chamber Group
- The Violin, Viola, Cello, and Bass books can be played and learned together.
- Warm up with the exercises and then play the fiddle tunes.
- Everyone can pick the part they feel most comfortable playing.
- Make sure at least one person is playing a melody part and at least one person is playing a harmony part. Feel free to play the teacher harmony part even if you are not a teacher!
- **The "A" and "B" parts of each exercise are compatible and can be played together.**
- **All melodies and harmonies for each fiddle tune are compatible and can be played together.**

Sample Order: How to Have Your Group Perform a Tune From This Book
Have students play the parts (A, B, etc.) listed for each time through the tune (1., 2., etc.)

| 1. A,B,C |
| 2. B,C |
| 3. A,C |

or

| 1. A,B,C,D |
| 2. B,C,D |
| 3. A,C,D |
| 4. A,B,C,D |

- Highlight the viola, cello, or bass parts by having everyone else play pizzicato on the harmony part.
- Performing with the piano accompaniment can help less-advanced groups center their intonation and stay together.

©2020 C. Harvey Publications All Rights Reserved.

1. Harvest Home: First Warm-Up

C. Harvey

A. Regular Exercise

B. Basic Exercise

©2020 C. Harvey Publications All Rights Reserved.

2. Harvest Home: Second Warm-Up

A. Regular Exercise

B. Basic Exercise

The Blackberry Blossom Fiddle Book for Bass

C. Basic Harmony

D. Teacher Harmony

pizz.

Note: Student repeat is written out.

©2020 C. Harvey Publications All Rights Reserved.

4. Blackberry Blossom: First Warm-Up

C. Harvey

A. Regular Exercise

B. Basic Exercise

©2020 C. Harvey Publications All Rights Reserved.

5. Blackberry Blossom: Second Warm-Up

A. Regular Exercise

B. Basic Exercise

6. Blackberry Blossom

The Blackberry Blossom Fiddle Book for Bass

Trad., arr. M. Harvey

A. Advanced Melody

B. Stress-Free Melody

©2020 C. Harvey Publications All Rights Reserved.

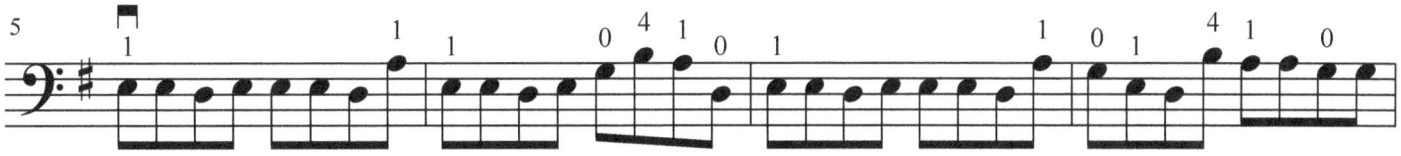

C. Basic Harmony

D. Teacher Harmony

pizz.

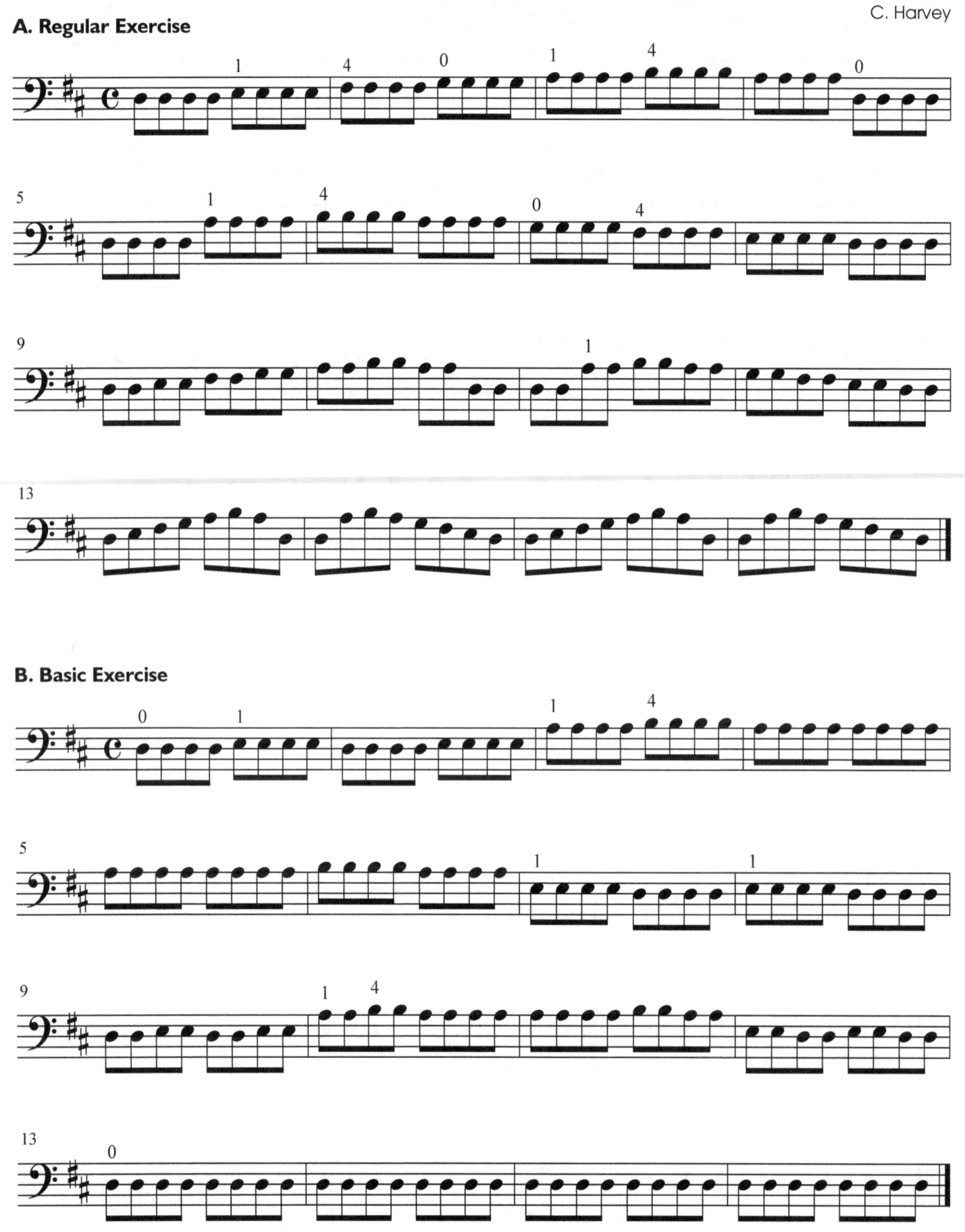

The Blackberry Blossom Fiddle Book for Bass 13

8. The Dashing Sergeant: Second Warm-Up

A. Regular Exercise

B. Basic Exercise

©2020 C. Harvey Publications All Rights Reserved.

The Blackberry Blossom Fiddle Book for Bass

C. Basic Harmony

D. Teacher Harmony

©2020 C. Harvey Publications All Rights Reserved.

10. Old Joe Clark: First Warm-Up

C. Harvey

A. Regular Exercise

B. Basic Exercise

©2020 C. Harvey Publications All Rights Reserved.

12. Old Joe Clark

The Blackberry Blossom Fiddle Book for Bass
Trad., arr. M. Harvey

A. Advanced Melody

B. Stress-Free Melody

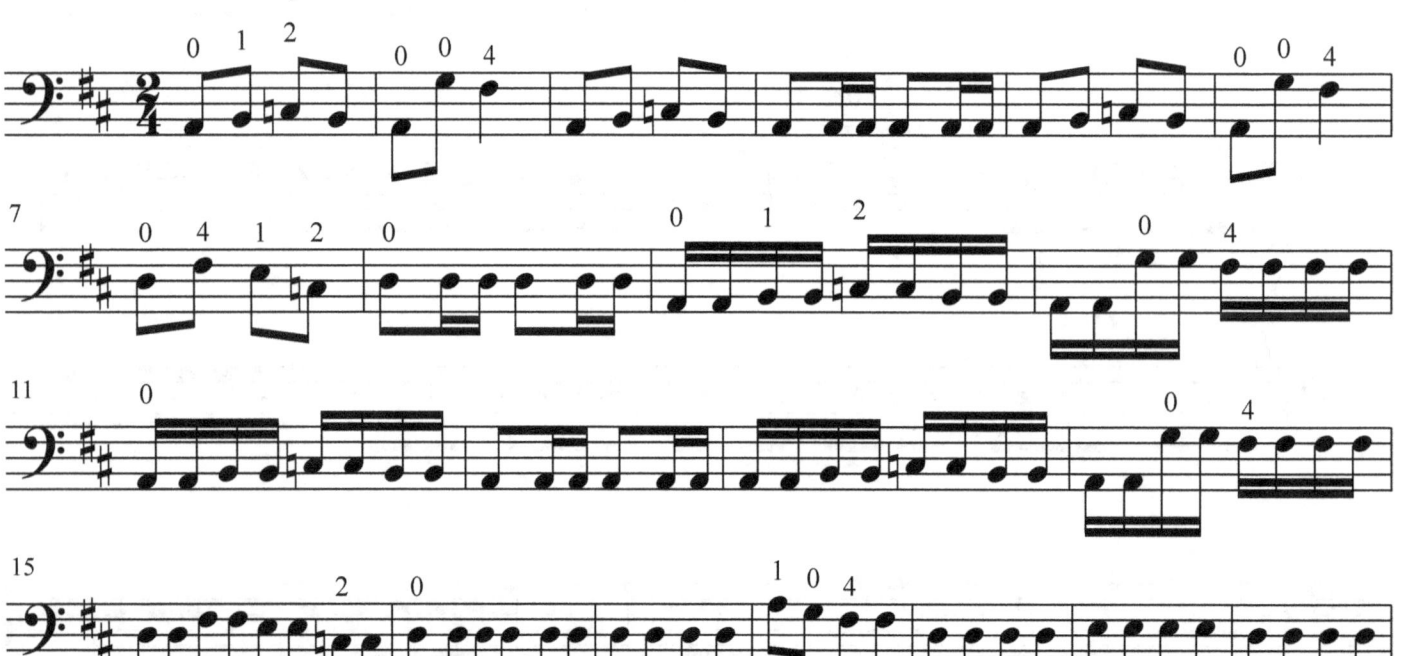

©2020 C. Harvey Publications All Rights Reserved.

13. King of the Fairies: First Warm-Up

C. Harvey

A. Regular Exercise

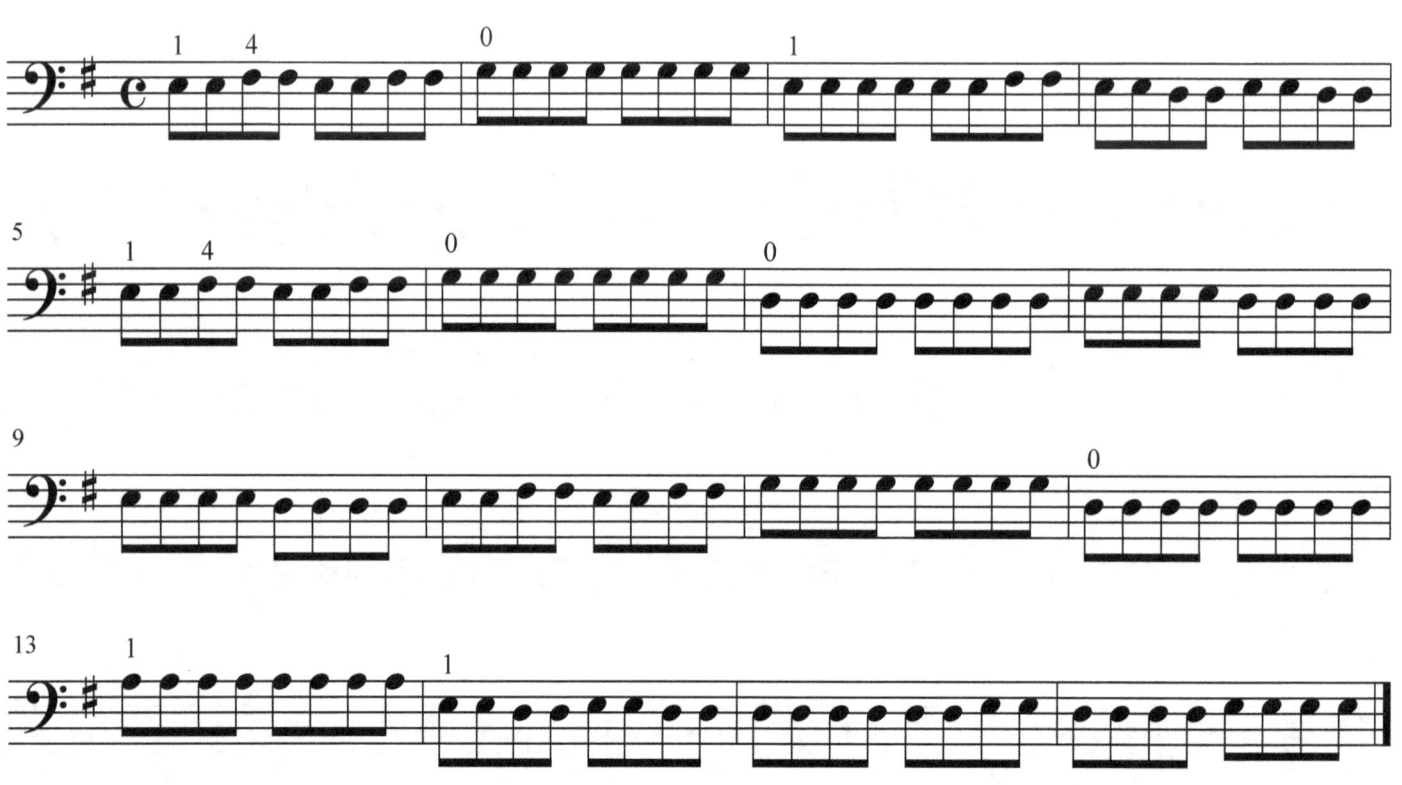

B. Basic Exercise

14. King of the Fairies: Second Warm-Up

A. Regular Exercise

B. Basic Exercise

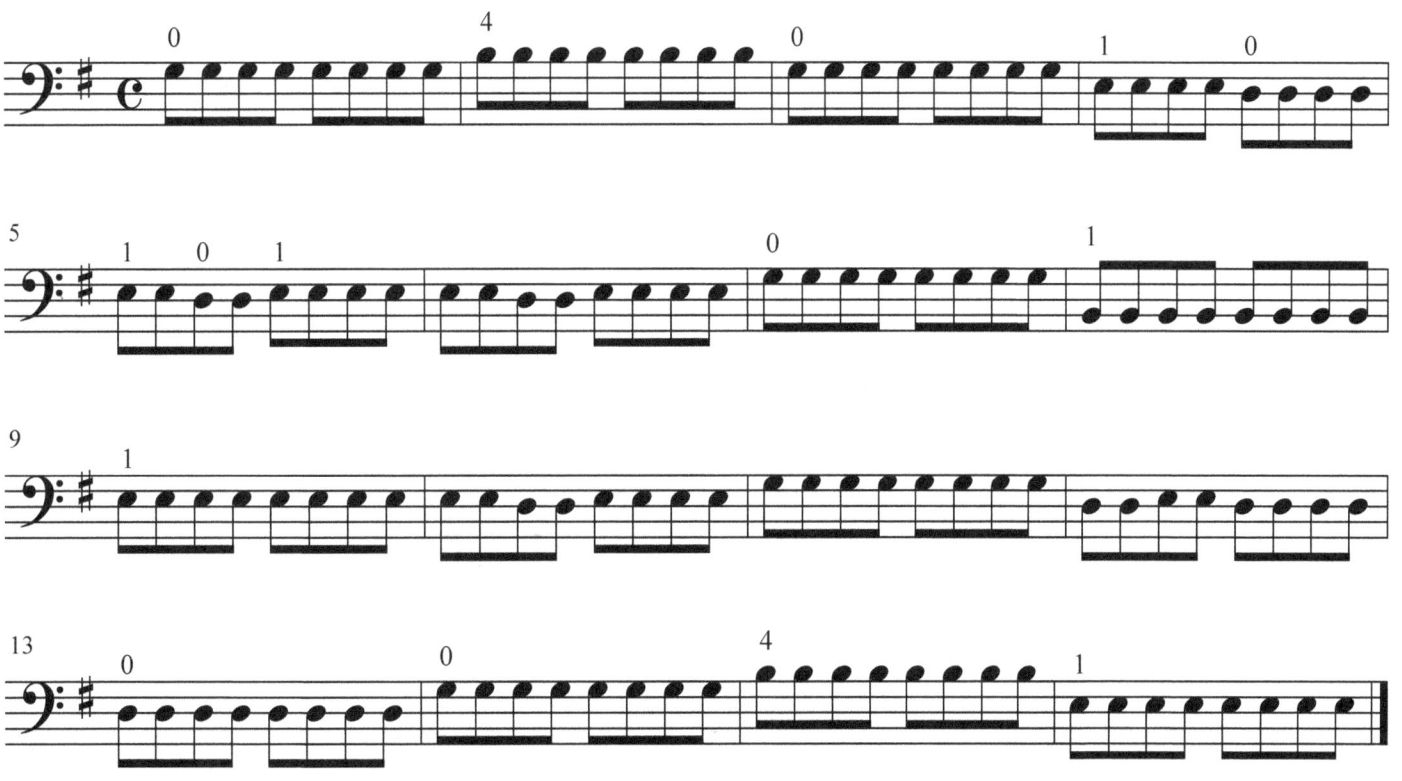

15. King of the Fairies

The Blackberry Blossom Fiddle Book for Bass
Trad., arr. M. Harvey

A. Advanced Melody

B. Stress-Free Melody

©2020 C. Harvey Publications All Rights Reserved.

C. Basic Harmony

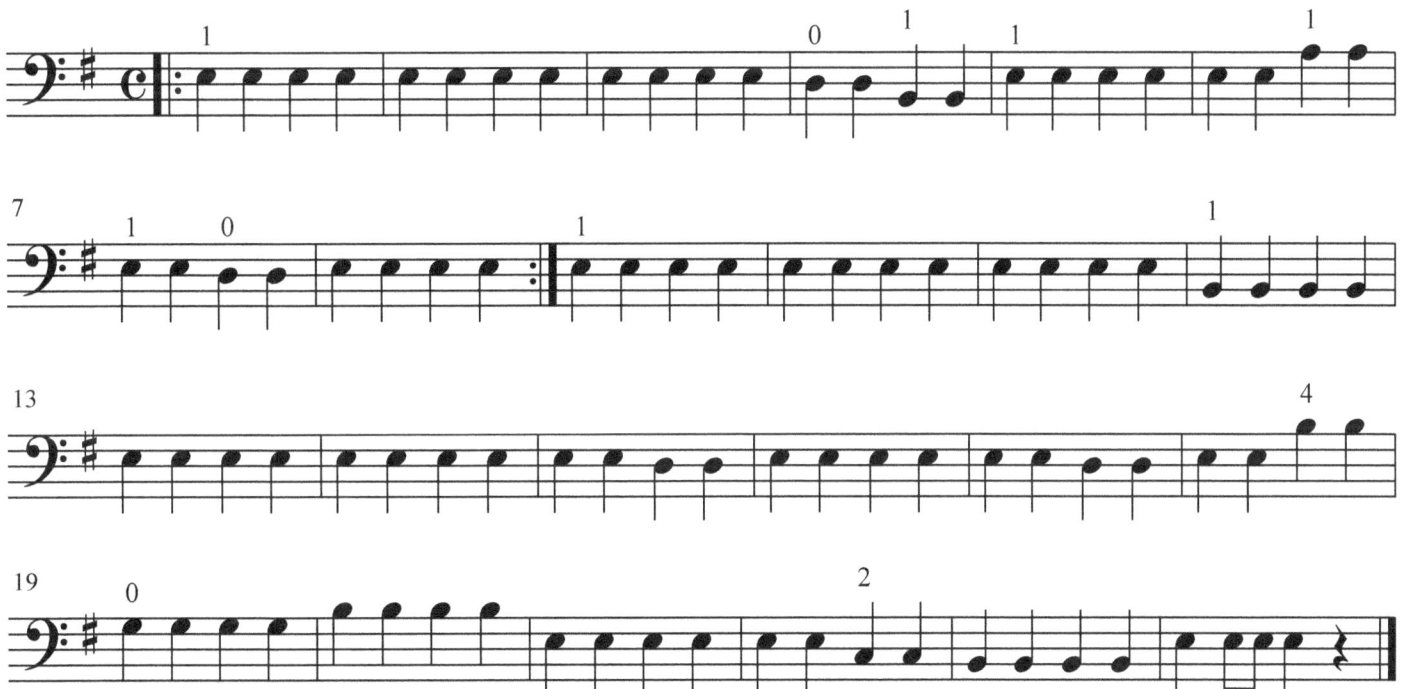

D. Teacher Harmony

16. Blarney Pilgrim: First Warm-Up

C. Harvey

©2020 C. Harvey Publications All Rights Reserved.

17. Blarney Pilgrim: Second Warm-Up

A. Regular Exercise

B. Basic Exercise

18. Blarney Pilgrim

The Blackberry Blossom Fiddle Book for Bass
Trad., arr. M. Harvey

A. Advanced Melody

B. Stress-Free Melody

©2020 C. Harvey Publications All Rights Reserved.

The Blackberry Blossom Fiddle Book for Bass

C. Basic Harmony

D. Teacher Harmony

©2020 C. Harvey Publications All Rights Reserved.

19. The Parting Blessing Warm-Up

C. Harvey

A. Regular Exercise

B. Basic Exercise

A. Advanced Melody
B. Stress-Free Melody

20. The Parting Blessing

Trad., arr. M. Harvey

The Blackberry Blossom Fiddle Book for Bass

C. Basic Harmony

D. Teacher Harmony

21. Leather Breeches: First Warm-Up

C. Harvey

A. Regular Exercise

B. Basic Exercise

22. Leather Breeches: Second Warm-Up

A. Regular Exercise

B. Basic Exercise

23. Leather Breeches

Trad., arr. M. Harvey

A. Advanced Melody

B. Stress-Free Melody

©2020 C. Harvey Publications All Rights Reserved.

C. Basic Harmony

D. Teacher Harmony

24. The Rakes of Kildare: First Warm-Up

C. Harvey

25. The Rakes of Kildare: Second Warm-Up

A. Regular Exercise

B. Basic Exercise

26. The Rakes of Kildare

Trad., arr. M. Harvey

A. Advanced Melody

B. Stress-Free Melody

©2020 C. Harvey Publications All Rights Reserved.

The Blackberry Blossom Fiddle Book for Bass

C. Basic Harmony

D. Teacher Harmony

pizz.

©2020 C. Harvey Publications All Rights Reserved.

27. Big John McNeil: First Warm-Up

C. Harvey

A. Regular Exercise

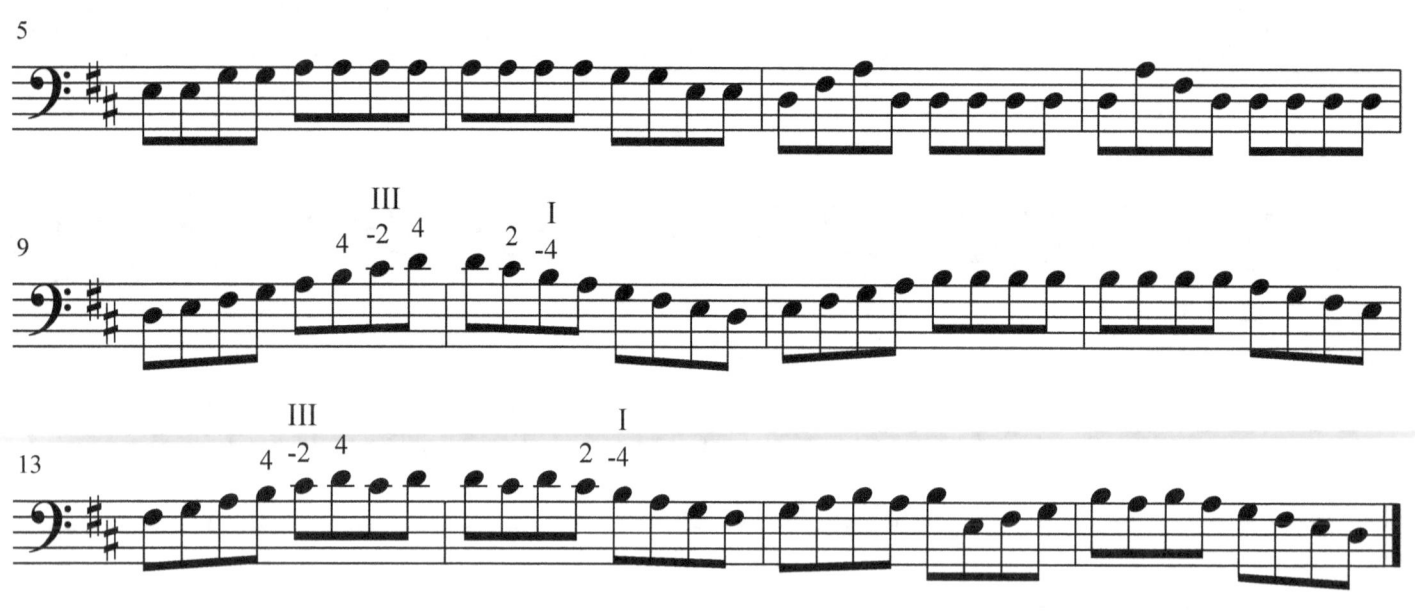

B. Basic Exercise

©2020 C. Harvey Publications All Rights Reserved.

28. Big John McNeil: Second Warm-Up

A. Regular Exercise

B. Basic Exercise

The Blackberry Blossom Fiddle Book for Bass

C. Basic Harmony

D. Teacher Harmony

©2020 C. Harvey Publications All Rights Reserved.

30. Red-Haired Boy: First Warm-Up

C. Harvey

A. Regular Exercise

B. Basic Exercise

31. Red-Haired Boy: Second Warm-Up

A. Regular Exercise

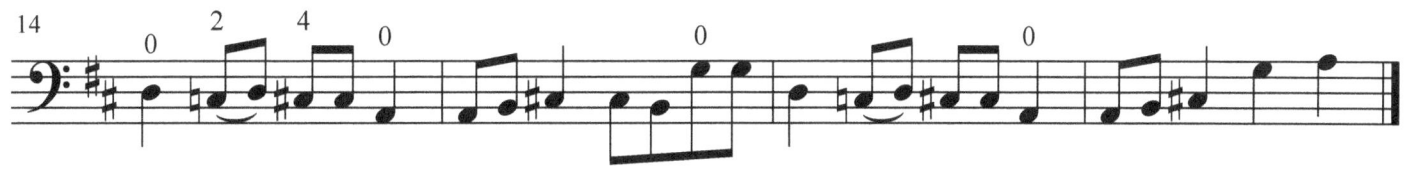

B. Basic Exercise

©2020 C. Harvey Publications All Rights Reserved.

32. Red-Haired Boy

Trad., arr. M. Harvey

A. Advanced Melody

B. Stress-Free Melody

©2020 C. Harvey Publications All Rights Reserved.

C. Basic Harmony

D. Teacher Harmony

PLAYING THE BASS, BOOK TWO
(FOR STRING CLASSES)

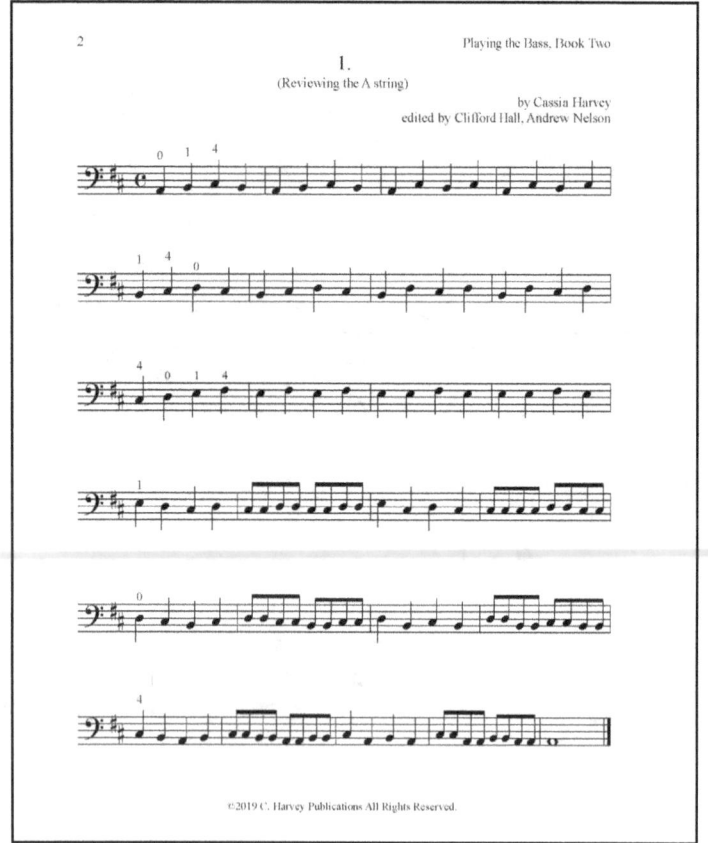 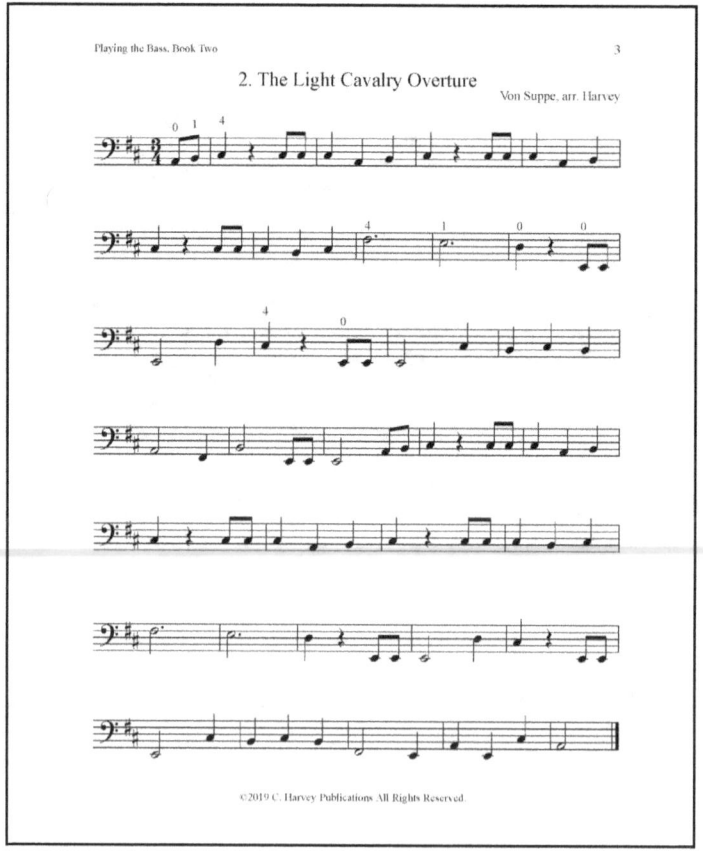

Fiddle fun and more!

This book helps bassists become more fluent in reading and playing music.

By combining short warm-up exercises with fun fiddle tunes and catchy classical pieces, the book can help your students build the skills they need for orchestra.

Tried and tested for years with hundreds of students, we can tell you definitively: this book makes playing fun!

Playing the Bass, Book Two can be used in mixed-string classes or studied on its own.

PLAYING THE VIOLIN, BOOK TWO CHP324
PLAYING THE VIOLA, BOOK TWO CHP325
PLAYING THE CELLO, BOOK TWO CHP326
PLAYING THE BASS, BOOK TWO CHP357

  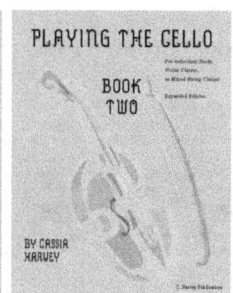 

WWW.CHARVEYPUBLICATIONS.COM

www.ingramcontent.com/pod-product-compliance
Lightning Source LLC
Chambersburg PA
CBHW081129080526
44587CB00021B/3801